Just Like Daddy

Lucy Freegard

PAVILION

My friends say that when they grow up, they want to be...

a ballet dancer,

an engineer,

For my daddy, who I love this much!

First published in the United Kingdom in 2017 by
Pavilion Children's Books
43 Great Ormond Street
London
WC1N 3HZ

An imprint of Pavilion Books Company Limited

Publisher and editor: Neil Dunnicliffe
Art director: Lee-May Lim

Layout © Pavilion Children's Books, 2017
Text and illustrations © Lucy Freegard, 2017

ISBN: 9781843653370

A CIP catalogue record for this book is available from the British Library

10 9 8 7 6 5 4 3 2 1

Reproduction by Colourdepth, UK
Printed by Toppan Leefung Printing Ltd, China

This book can be ordered directly from the publisher online at www.pavilionbooks.com
or try your local bookshop.

and a pirate.

But when I grow up,

I want
to be...

...just like Daddy!

I will be brave enough
to deal with the
scariest of monsters,

and daring enough
to keep my eyes wide open
on the twistiest of rollercoasters

(even when I **really** want to close them).

I will be smart enough to build a special place to play.

And when I tell stories,
I will put on all
the silly voices.

When I'm as big as Daddy,
I will be strong enough to win at tug-of-war,

and go as *fast* as the wind.

I will climb to the top of the tallest mountains and be only a teeny bit out of breath.

When I grow up,
I will have the
best memories.

Daddy says he'll miss
the little me;

even my grumpy days,

cheeky moments,

and terrible tantrums.

Everyone says I'm growing up fast.

But Daddy says that he will always love me,
no matter what.

Daddy says **nobody** is perfect.

We **all** make mistakes sometimes.

But you're never too old
(or too young) to try something silly.

My daddy still loves...

sand building,

facepaint,

and, best of all...

...birthdays!

Because no matter how **big** he is...

...my daddy still remembers

how much fun it is to be little,

just like me!